The Fire Maker's Manual

70+ Ways to Get Your Fire Started

By: Tristan Trouble

Published in USA by:

CDI Publications, LLC
P.O BOX #9
Boynton Beach
FL 33425

© Copyright 2018

ISBN-13: 978-1717344281
ISBN-10: 1717344283

Table of Contents

4

Fire as a Survival Skill

49

Introduction

The importance of fire in a survival situation cannot be overstated. Having the ability to start a fire and maintain it safely, is a skill set that can literally save your life. In the emergency preparedness industry, we live by the "rule of threes," which states that the average healthy human being can live for up to 3 minutes without oxygen, 3 hours without shelter, 3 days without water, and up to 3 weeks without food. In the absence of shelter, a properly built fire can extend that time frame indefinitely.

In a real world, life or death situation, fire can provide us with many of the benefits we take for granted in our normal day-to-day lives. The mere sight of a fire can trigger pleasant memories of sitting around campfires roasting hotdogs on a stick or making S'mores as a child. As mentioned above, a fire can also provide warmth, which is absolutely essential if a shelter is unavailable, or needs to be built.

Fire also gives us the ability to boil water, purifying it and making it safe for human consumption, as well as using it for personal hygiene. Unpurified water can contain harmful organisms, which if consumed can result in severe illness and/or death. While not as prevalent in the United States, waterborne diseases remain a leading cause of death on the international scene.

Fire lets us cook food, which can help us obtain a sense of normalcy in an otherwise unsavory situation. While some wild edibles can be eaten raw, animals must be cooked to ensure it is safe for human consumption. Raw animal flesh may contain harmful organisms, which if consumed may have fatal results.

Fire provides us with light, which helps us see better during low light and dark conditions, and that alone can help keep us from getting injured while moving around at night. Having the ability to see also allows us to continue performing tasks and duties that would otherwise have to wait until sun rise the following day.

A fire will also serve as a warning sign to passing animals and those in the surrounding vicinity, which should keep predatory beasts at bay. Should animals approach, a dead branch can be converted into a torch and used to steer the animal away. This should not however be your sole source of defense against aggressive wildlife.

Most survival situations include the need for rescue, and fire can make this easier to achieve as well by acting as a signaling device. Even the glow from a small fire can be seen from a great distance. The easier you are to see and the more visibility you can provide for your position, the better chance you have of being rescued.

Fire even serves us to a lesser degree by acting as an insect repellant. It also gives us a method for sterilizing medical utensils and can be used to keep clothes dry, or to dry those that become wet. As an added bonus, fire produces ash and charcoal, both of which can be extremely useful in a long term situation; ashes from a fire can be used to make lye soap, and charcoal can be used for several things, such as camouflage, water filtration, and as an anti-diarrheal medicine, just to name a few.

Fire Making Elements & Materials

Before we get into how to actually start a fire, perhaps we should take a few moments to discuss the elements that are required to ignite a fire and keep it going. This information may be useful if you are having difficulty getting a fire lit. There are three elements that must be present in order for fire to occur;

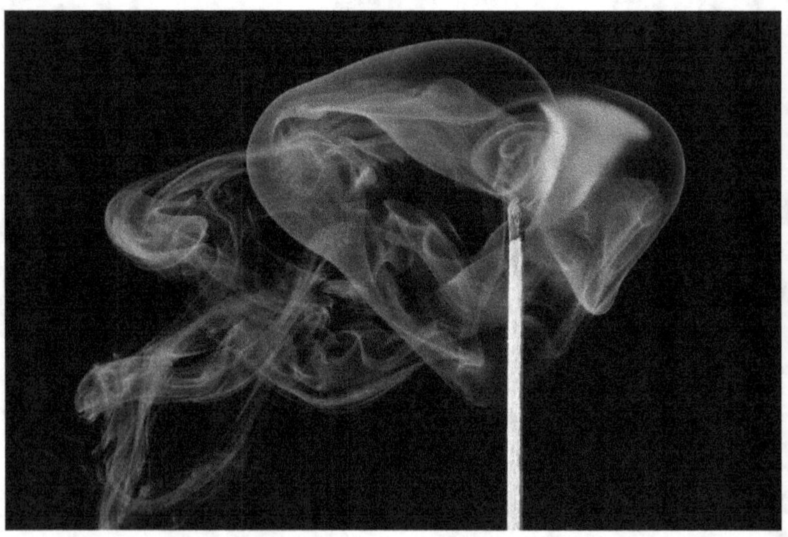

Elements

- ➢ **Oxygen -** this is the by far the easiest element to find when trying to make a fire. Oxygen is abundant and is also an element required for life; it exists in the air that surrounds us. On average, air normally contains approximately 21% oxygen; fire requires a bare minimum of 16% oxygen in order to burn and stay lit. Oxygen assists the chemical processes that take place when a fire burns. When the fuel of the fire starts to burn, it interacts with the oxygen content present in the surrounding air by releasing heat and combustible byproducts, such as smoke, gas, and sparks; this is known as oxidation.

- ➢ **Fuel -** is another element that is required to start a fire. Without fuel a spark is about all you will be able to generate. Fuel for a fire consists of any material that is considered combustible. Fuel for a fire comes in many different sizes, shapes, and quantities; it may also have moisture content. The amount of moisture present in the fuel will determine just how easily it ignites and how quickly it burns. New fuel must be continuously added to a fire as previous fuel sources are exhausted by the burning process, otherwise the fire will die out.

- ➢ **Heat -** this is an element that may be very easy to come by, or one that is extremely difficult to produce. Heat is the element that is directly responsible for igniting the fire. It is also required to enable the fire to spread. It does this by drying out any fuel in close proximity, which makes the fuel easier for the fire to consume.

If any of the elements above are missing, the fire will not only be difficult to start, it will be all but impossible to maintain. Fire occurs rather easily when all of the elements are available and mixed in the right combination. In reverse fashion, a fire is extinguished by removing one or more of the elements; this is rather easy to accomplish in a controlled environment but is extremely difficult to achieve when the fire spreads to an environment where control of the elements is not possible, such as a wildfire.

Now that we have an understanding of the elements required to get a fire going, let's take a few minutes to look over the raw materials we will most likely find in the wilderness that will make starting a fire easier to achieve. It is important to note that although we are covering raw materials in this section, several conventional materials can also be used in place of raw materials, should a fire need to be started close to home, such as in the backyard, or a burn barrel.

Raw Materials

The materials required to get a fire going can also be characterized into three categories. While it may be possible to get a fire going without all of these materials present, it will be much easier to accomplish if these materials are present and arranged accordingly to assist and support the act of building a fire;

> **Tinder** - refers to material that is easy to ignite. Tinder represents the smallest of the materials required to make a fire. It is also highly combustible and should catch fire with little more than a spark

from a heat source. Shredded cotton balls, cattail fluff, lint from clothing or a dryer, and dry grass and leaves are examples of tinder that are normally available or easy to produce in an outdoor environment when starting a fire is of the utmost importance.

➤ **Kindling** - refers to material that is slightly larger than tinder, yet still dry, combustible, and easy to get burning. This material will not ignite from a spark; it must be introduced to a flame long enough for the fire to take hold. Tree bark, small twigs, pine cones, etc. are examples that fall into the kindling category. This material will make up the second layer of a fire configuration and should consist of slightly more material than the tinder layer.

➤ **Firewood -** refers to dry, combustible material that is as big around as the arm of an average adult human. Tree branches and tree trunks from hardwood trees are preferred for this category as they will burn the longest and the cleanest. This material serves as the main fuel of the fire and requires a strong flame to get going. It needs to be added periodically to keep the fire going.

Now that we've covered that topic, it bears stating that there is a method to the madness of starting a fire. For example, most fire configurations call for the base to consist of tinder, the next layer consists of kindling, and the final layer contains the firewood; the inverted fire configuration arranges these layers in reverse fashion.

Conventional fire configurations are arranged with the tinder at the bottom, followed by the kindling, then the firewood so that the fire is easier to start and get going. Conventional fire configurations also help prevent problems when starting a fire by having all the material readily available in a confined and controlled environment. While it is possible to light the tinder, add the kindling, then top it off with firewood, this process involves the potential for problems to appear, such as the fire burning out before enough fuel has been added to keep the fire going.

Common Fire Configurations

Now that we have a firm grasp in the elements and materials required to make fire, let's touch base on a couple of the more common fire configurations we can use to our advantage when trying to light a fire. The fire configurations listed in this section are those that should be easy to replicate in a survival situation; where possible images have been included for clarity.

Tepee Configuration

The image above depicts the traditional tepee fire configuration. The tinder is placed in the middle of the fire base. This tinder ball is surrounded with kindling that is arranged in an inverted cone shape. The kindling is then surrounded by the logs that will be used as fuel for the fire, which is arranged in the shape of a tepee, hence the name.

Space is left in between the twigs and branches that make up the kindling and the firewood. This allows for better airflow which delivers the required oxygen to the fire once it is lit. This spacing also allows the fire builder to place an ignition source or spark onto the tinder to get the fire started. This is one of the easiest fire configurations to replicate in the wilderness.

Log Cabin Configuration

The image above depicts a log cabin fire configuration. In essence, this formation is a tepee fire configuration that is surrounded by a log cabin type structure of additional firewood. The tepee configuration mentioned previously above is laid out, then two larger logs are placed parallel to one another on opposite sides of the tepee configuration. This build process continues by placing slightly smaller logs parallel to each other, yet perpendicular to the layer below, as you would with a log cabin.

The log cabin build process continues until the

configuration reaches the height desired. Again, spaces are left in between the logs of the log cabin as well as the tepee, allowing the fire to be started and to ensure proper airflow. This is another very simple fire configuration that is easy to replicate with materials found in nature.

Pyramid Configuration

The image above depicts what a pyramid fire configuration stack looks like. This configuration calls for laying the tinder and kindling at the middle of the fire base. The first two logs of the pyramid are arranged parallel to each other on opposite sides of the tinder and kindling. The ascending layers of the pyramid are then laid out as they are in the image above. This creates an air gap at the base of the fire that allows the tinder and kindling to be lit.

This configuration is a bit more difficult to arrange in the wilderness; however, it will burn much longer than the previous two configurations mentioned and will create a fire put of embers that can be used to create charcoal, or to start another fire should the fuel of the original burn down.

Inverted Pyramid Configuration

This fire configuration basically consists of building the pyramid fire configuration without the air gap at the bottom; all layers of firewood are arranged as in the image above, including the ground layer. The kindling is then layered on top of the pyramid and a tinder ball is placed in the center and lit. As the tinder ball catches flame it will ignite the kindling below, which if arranged properly will burn a hole down through the center of the pyramid while simultaneously spreading to the outer edges.

This is a very long burning fire when built properly,

which in a survival situation will allow you to conduct other important tasks without having to tend the fire every few minutes. While this may be a more complex configuration to master, build it right once and the benefits will be more than obvious.

These are the recommended fire configurations to become familiar with, especially for those who are just developing their fire making skills. Each of these configurations can be achieved with minimal effort, some more minimal than others, using average sized firewood as the fuel. One should strive to master using these fire configurations before attempting to build configurations designed to be self-feeding, or which require much bigger logs for firewood.

75 Ways to Start a Fire

If you're newly developing your fire making skills, then you may be surprised to discover that there are several ways to get a fire going. Some of the methods we are going to cover in this manual are conventional and common; they will be easy for you to recognize and associate with. In fact, there's a better than average chance you've either used a few of these conventional methods yourself, or you've seen others use them successfully.

Other methods are going to be of the unconventional variety; they will be difficult for you to recognize and may even border on the unbelievable. However, each of the methods mentioned here have been tested and proven possible; that isn't to say they are easy to achieve or that they will work for you. Some of these unconventional methods will rely heavily on environmental factors, such as sunlight, which isn't always available even during day time hours.

Conventional Methods of Making Fire

The methods listed in this category utilize items readers should be familiar with. These are items that have been used to make fire for centuries. Some of these methods are not traditionally used to make fire, but readers should still be able to associate them with the ability to start a fire.

Conventional methods either use items manufactured specifically for making fire, such as a standard butane lighter, or they use items that the reader will quickly recognize as capable of lighting a fire.

Solar Based

The fire making methods in this category make use of the sun by concentrating rays of sunlight onto a central focal point. The concentrated rays from the sun will provide the heat required to start a fire provided they are focused on combustible material in the form of tinder.

- ➤ **Magnifying Glass** - for magnifying glasses to work they must be fairly free from scratches. If you cannot see clearly through the lens, it may not concentrate rays from the sun well enough to get a fire going. Magnifying glasses that are in good condition simply need to be held between the tinder and the sun at the proper interval, which is accomplished by moving the glass closer to, or further from, the tinder ball until such a time as the rays from the sun are focused into the smallest possible point of light. That point of light is then aimed directly at the tinder ball and held there until it lights the tinder on fire.
- ➤ **Fresnel Lens** - this is basically a curved lens that has been flattened by dividing the curve into smaller segments. These lenses work in similar fashion to a magnifying glass and may be easier to carry in an emergency preparedness kit or GO bag.
- ➤ **Parabolic Reflector** - also referred to as a solar cigarette lighter, this device uses a small curved dish

(think of it as a miniature chrome plated satellite dish) that concentrates sunlight on a given focal point. This can be used to get a tinder ball ignited, after which the tinder will need to be transported and placed in the fire pit.

Spark Based

The methods for making fire in this category require the creation of a spark. The spark is then captured in a ball of tinder where it can be teased into a dancing flame. The flame is then transferred to the kindling where it can consume enough fuel to light the larger logs of firewood.

Some of the methods in this category use devices that not only create the spark, but are also able to produce a flame, which can then be used to ignite the tinder into a flame that will spread to the kindling and then onto the firewood.

> **Ferro Rod Fire Starters** - often misidentified as "magnesium" fire starters, ferrocerium is a metal alloy that consists of iron, cerium, and lanthanum, with less than 2% magnesium added to the mix. A ferro rod will give off sparks when scratched with a hardened object, such as carbon steel. Ferro rods can be used to ignite tinder, flammable accelerants, and magnesium shavings.

> **Magnesium Rods** - these devices are generally solid magnesium, which when shaved will produce a small pile of filings that can then be ignited using a ferro rod, flint and steel, or any other spark producing piece of gear.

> Permanent Match - this device is often coupled with a keychain allowing you to carry it with you everywhere. It consists of a small metal matchstick with a replaceable wick that is housed in a small metal container which has a ferro rod attached to the side; it is also refillable. The wick of the match is

saturated with lighter fluid which ignites rather easily when scratched down the ferro rod on the outer edge.

> **<u>Blast Match</u>** - this is a flint based device that can be used with a single hand. The blast match can generate sparks for up to 4,000 strikes, all of which can be targeted to a specific area, such as a tinder ball. It works in wet weather and has safety features that prevent accidental sparking when not in use.

> **<u>Spark-Lite</u>** - this is a fire starting kit that allows for easy use with a single hand. It basically consists of a flint and a sparking wheel similar to those found in Zippo lighters. As the wheel is rotated against the flint a shower of sparks is created, which can be directed towards a tinder ball to ignite a flame and get a fire going.

Compression Based

When it comes to compression based fire making methods, the fire piston reigns supreme. In fact, fire pistons are essentially the only compression based method for making fire. Although fire pistons and compression based fire making methods may sound new to you, they have been around for several centuries.

The first reported fire piston in the West was created as a by-product of air guns. Abbot Agostino Ruffo from

Verona, Italy stumbled upon the invention while testing the pump of an air gun he had built for Portugal's King John V. Ruffo plugged the outlet of an air gun with wooden scraps then pressurized the pump. When he later removed the wood, he discovered it was scorched. This led to a later discovery that the pump could ignite tinder.

Fire pistons can be manufactured models, or they can be <u>DIY designs</u>. In either case they use the same principle for compressing air and heating it rapidly. It should be noted that DIY fire pistons can be made out of an abundance of materials, such as bamboo, PVC pipe, clear acrylic, metallic flashlight bodies, etc.

> ➤ <u>Fire Piston</u>—a fire piston works by rapidly compressing a gas (air in this case), which causes an increase in pressure and temperature simultaneously. If the fire piston is operated fast enough the temperature of the air will rapidly increase until it is hot enough to ignite tinder.

Firearm Based

Believe it or not, there are several methods of making fire that come from this category. While this isn't necessarily the safest method for making a fire, if you have the means it may come in handy during a survival situation.

Some of the methods mentioned in this category involve the use of ammunition alone, a few of which are considered "exotic" ammunitions, whereas other methods make use of the firearm and ammunition together.

> **Gunpowder** - can be removed from most, if not all, conventional cartridges. It will be much easier to remove the gunpowder from a shotgun shell than it will be to remove it from a rifle/pistol cartridge. Once removed the gunpowder can be ground down even further to produce a larger surface area which

should improve the odds of getting a spark to light the gunpowder.

- ➢ **Cloth Wad Shotgun Shells -** this is a secondary method for making fire that requires the use of a shotgun. This process calls for removing the front end of a shotgun shell, then removing the shot, wadding, and gunpowder. A small cotton cloth is then covered in gunpowder, rolled up and packed back into the empty shotgun shell. The shell is loaded into the shotgun and fired as normal. The burning cloth will exit the barrel of the shotgun, after which it can be retrieved. The cloth wad should be fired in a safe direction and at a distance it will be easy to retrieve and/or transport to the tinder and kindling.
- ➢ **Signal Flares -** believe it or not, there are signal flares that are designed as shotgun shells. A signal flare will fire out the end of the barrel much faster than a gunpowder coated cloth wad, so you may need to fire it in a direction that will make it easier to retrieve. Signal flares should not be shot directly into a fire pit as they could ricochet and result in damage or an uncontrollable fire.
- ➢ **Incendiary Ammunition -** although illegal to sell, purchase, or own in several states, incendiary ammunition, such as "Dragon's Breath," is available for several types of firearms, including rifles, shotguns, and hand guns. This ammunition is designed specifically for the purpose of starting a fire. When shot from a firearm, this ammunition emits an enormous number of sparks, which ignite fire when coming into contact with combustible materials.

Other Conventional Methods

The fire making methods mentioned in the categories above may not seem as conventional as those listed in this category; however, when all of these methods are compared to the unconventional methods it will become apparent how much easier these methods are to use when trying to make it out of a survival situation alive.

You will be able to recognize most of the fire making methods mentioned in this category. In fact, most of us will have at least one of these fire making methods available in our emergency preparedness kits, EDC (Every Day Carry), or both. Some of us may even use one or more of these methods on a daily basis.

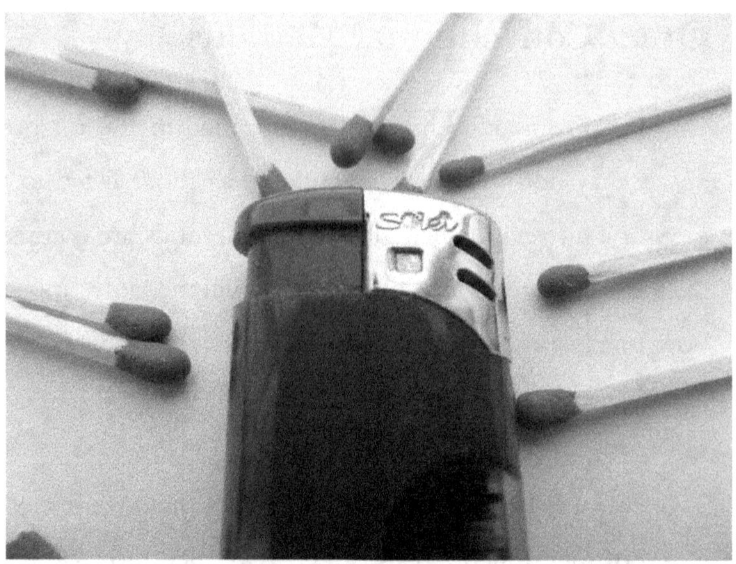

➢ **Matches** - believe it or not, matchbooks are still manufactured and distributed, which means you can pick them up from a number of suppliers. Some grocery store chains will carry them, certain cigarette outlets and smoke shops will have them, and they can even be ordered online from various merchants. High quality paper matches will be easy to use, whereas the cheap quality paper matches may crumble and be difficult to use. Paper matches have to be struck against the striker strip available on the back of the matchbook in order to spark and catch fire.

➢ **Waterproof Matches** - are more preferable than standard paper matches of any quality, for obvious reasons; they can be lit even after they have been subjected to moisture. This is a huge benefit when trying to get a fire going in a wet and miserable environment. Waterproof matches are often stored in a water tight container that incorporates the striker strip for the matches. It is highly recommended that you have waterproof matches in your emergency preparedness kits, if for no other reason than as a wet weather back-up for the method you prefer.

➢ **Strike Anywhere Matches -** generally have a wooden stick body. The head of the match contains a material called perchlorate. This material makes the match suitable for striking against any surface where friction can be created. In order for a surface to be suitable for creating friction, it must be somewhat rough, but not too rough. Smooth surfaces, such as glass, will not be suitable for use with strike anywhere matches.

➢ **Improvised Matchbook Igniters -** this method calls for igniting all of the matches in a paper matchbook simultaneously. This creates a much larger flame than a single match and allows for faster ignition of the tinder ball and kindling. This method may come in handy for breezy environments, or to dry out and ignite slightly damp tinder. It should not be used if the paper matchbook happens to be the last method of making a fire, as it could consume the rest of your fire making methods and leave you stranded without fire.

➢ **Zippo Lighters -** if you're not sure what a Zippo lighter looks like, take a few minutes to research Google images and become familiar with them. Zippo lighters will work in several conditions, including in the wet and windy wilderness. Zippo lighters are refillable and repairable, which makes them a welcome addition to the GO bag.

> **Butane Lighters** - are available at almost every corner convenience store in America; they are usually located on the counter next to the cash register. These lighters are considered disposable but will serve to light several fires before the fluid runs dry, and even after the fluid is empty, the lighter itself may still be useful for getting a fire going.

> **Empty Lighters** - this refers to both Zippo and disposable butane models. When empty, these lighters still have friction wheels and flints that can be used to generate enough sparks to ignite a small ball of dry tinder.

> **Carbide Lamps** - are devices that use calcium carbide to generate a flame. These lamps are most often used by spelunkers (cave explorers). The carbide lamps have a water filled chamber that allows a trickle of water to drip onto carbide lumps which are held in a separate chamber beneath the water. This creates a gas that is allowed to escape through an exit tube after which it is lit by a sparking mechanism. This is not a device most of us will carry; however, if you have one or come across one, you can start a fire with it.

> **Road Flares** - these devices are slow burning. Think of road flares as safety matches on steroids; the ends and caps of road flares are covered with the same stuff found on safety match heads. Once lit, a road flare will burn long enough to help dry tinder and kindling, as well as get the fire going.

> **Signal Flares/Flare Guns** - are very similar to the road flares described above. Handheld signal flares

function just like road flares; however, aerial signal flares must be shot from a flare gun. Both can be used to make fire in a survival situation. Use extreme caution if using a flare gun. The flare must be shot towards the ground and retrieved without causing a wildfire.

- **Micro Butane Torches** - are available from several distributors. They can usually be found in hardware stores or from online merchants. Similar to butane lighters, torches generate a focused flame in the form of a jet stream which makes it much easier to get a fire going.
- **Propane Torches** - are similar to butane torches only larger. They operate on a different fuel source (propane) which is contained in a disposable cylinder. These torches produce a jet stream of fire that will make lighting the fire easier to accomplish.
- **Cutting/Welding Torches** - are not devices that most of us will have available to us in a survival situation. However, not all disasters will take place in the wilderness; if/when they occur in populated regions, cutting/welding torches may be found in industrial sectors. These torches often require a separate ignition source to generate a flame, but they can help you get a fire going.
- **Cutting/Welding Torch Ignitors** - are spark producing devices normally used to light a cutting/welding torch. They are handheld spring loaded devices with replaceable flints that can be used to ignite dry tinder. Think of them as being similar to empty lighters that are still able to generate sparks.
- **Electric Cigarette Lighters** - are available from several retailers. Similar to gas filled lighters, these

devices are small, handheld items that can be used to ignite tinder. Instead of using fuel, these devices use small wire coils that glow when the button is activated. These glowing coils can be used to light tinder, which can then be transferred to a fire pit containing kindling and larger fuel logs.

➢ **Vehicle Lighters -** are larger examples of the electric cigarette lighters. They are available in select vehicles and function by pressing them in and waiting for them to pop out. The glowing coils can then be used to ignite a bundle of tinder and kindling.

➢ **9 Volt Battery & Steel Wool -** this method calls for steel wool to be spread out near the tinder and kindling. The posts of the 9 volt battery are then raked across the steel wool which will cause sparks to generate and the steel wool to catch fire. Several similar examples of this method will also work; standard cell batteries (AA, AAA, C, D) and aluminum foil can also be used to generate a small flame and get a fire going; the aluminum foil is touched to the positive and negative posts of the battery which will cause the foil to super heat and catch fire.

Unconventional Methods of Making Fire

The methods of making fire listed in this category may use items that the reader is vaguely familiar with; these items are generally not available for purchase from a merchant. Most of these methods consist of DIY devices and designs that have been used throughout history to help man control the manufacturing of fire.

Several of the methods mentioned under this heading are similar to one another; they use the same device but with the assistance of things the reader may not have thought of themselves. In a survival situation, the ability to get a fire going will be a significant factor in successful survival.

Solar Based

The fire making methods in this category make use of the sun by concentrating rays of sunlight onto a central focal point. The concentrated rays from the sun will provide the heat required to start a fire provided they are focused on combustible material in the form of tinder.

- ➤ **Clear Glass/Acrylic Spheres -** these devices are generally sold as lawn ornaments, or as décor around the house. They function in similar fashion as magnifying lenses by concentrating the rays of the sun onto a central focal point. These focused rays can be used to ignite tinder for a fire.
- ➤ **Reading Glasses -** have lenses that can also be used to focus the rays of the sun onto a central focal point. Reading glasses are basically magnifying lenses that are much cheaper than prescription glasses. These devices can be purchased from grocery store chains and pharmacies for a fair price and should be added to your GO bags as a backup fire starter, if nothing else.
- ➤ **Binoculars -** are devices that many of us will have in our bugout gear. Aim the larger lenses towards the sun and the smaller eye lenses at the tinder bundle and the sun will be concentrated on a central

focal point; this is where the tinder should be located.

➤ **Monocular -** this is a device that is very similar to binoculars; the biggest difference being that there is only a single lens to look through. These devices can be used in the same fashion as binoculars to concentrate the rays of the sun onto a central focal point, such as a ball of tinder to get a fire going.

➤ **Spotting Scope -** is a device that is normally used to spot game at a distance; however, they can also be used in the same fashion as the two listed directly above to focus rays from the sun onto a central point where the tinder bundle is located.

➤ **Telescope -** while most of us won't have one of these devices in our GO bag, if disaster strikes close to home, we might have one of these scopes in the closet that could come in handy for getting a fire started.

➤ **Rifle Scope -** readers should be able to recognize this type of device. The scope should be removed from the rifle before being used to make a fire. The scope is arranged in similar fashion to that of the binoculars/monocular/scopes listed above, which focuses the rays of the sun onto a tinder bundle.

➤ **Clear Bottle w/Water -** any clear bottle, glass or plastic, filled with clear water can be converted into a fire making device. One end of the bottle must have a rounded surface in order for this method to work. Place water in the bottle and use the rounded surface to focus the rays of the sun onto the desired central point where the tinder bundle is located.

➤ **Clear Balloon w/Water -** clear balloons are difficult to find but not impossible. They can be used in similar fashion as the clear water bottle described above to focus rays of the sun where they need to be in order to make fire.

- ➤ **Clear Plastic Bag w/Water** - clear plastic bags are something all of us should have in our GO gear as they can be used for several things. When filled with water they can be used to grab rays from the sun and focus them onto a central point to get a fire going.
- ➤ **Clear Condom w/Water** - just like a clear plastic bag filled with water, a clear condom can also be used to focus rays from the sun when filled with water. Clear condoms can also be used for several things in a survival situation, making them a useful inclusion in any emergency preparedness kit.
- ➤ **Clear Incandescent Light Bulb w/Water** - these may not be something we have with us in the wilderness. However, should disaster strike while we're at home, there's a good chance we will be able to locate one of these devices in a pinch. The threaded end of the bulb must be removed using caution and safety. The bulb is then filled with water and used like several of the methods mentioned above.
- ➤ **Clear Plastic w/Water** - a clear sheet of plastic, or even plastic wrap, can be fashioned into a bag, filled with water, and used in the same fashion as those methods mentioned directly above. This may be a little more difficult to accomplish, but it is doable in a pinch.
- ➤ **Clear Wine Glass w/Water** - wine glasses often have a rounded surface that makes them an excellent unconventional device for making fire. Water is poured into the glass and it is held like a

bottle of water to direct the rays of the sun onto a central focal point where the tinder is located.

➤ **DIY Parabolic Reflectors -** these are devices and items that are used together to create a makeshift parabolic reflector. Tinder bundles must be held in position by something that is not flammable or combustible in order to get them to ignite.

- o **Satellite Dish & Tinfoil -** the satellite dish has a rounded surface that can be covered with tin foil and used to capture rays from the sun and focus them at a known central point. Tinder bundles must be placed where the sun's rays are concentrated and once ignited they must be transported to the fire pit where kindling and fuel awaits
- o **Stainless Steel Kitchen Bowl -** has a very smooth and shiny surface. It simply needs to be placed in the proper position to capture and focus rays from the sun.
- o **Regular Bowl & Tinfoil -** the interior of the bowl is lined with tinfoil and the makeshift parabolic reflector is used as described above.
- o **Aluminum Beverage Can Bottom -** this method will require the user to polish the bottom of the can, making it shiny and reflective enough to capture and focus rays from the sun onto a central point.
- o **Stainless Steel Soup Ladle -** has the same shape and configuration as a stainless steel kitchen bowl but on a much smaller scale.
- o **Flashlight Reflector -** this device must be removed from the flashlight before it can be used as a makeshift parabolic reflector, but

flashlights are something all of us should have in our GO gear, so they may come in handy in a pinch.

Spark Based

The methods for making fire in this category require the creation of a spark. The spark is then captured in a ball of tinder where it can be teased into a dancing flame. The flame is then transferred to the kindling where it can consume enough fuel to light the larger logs of firewood.

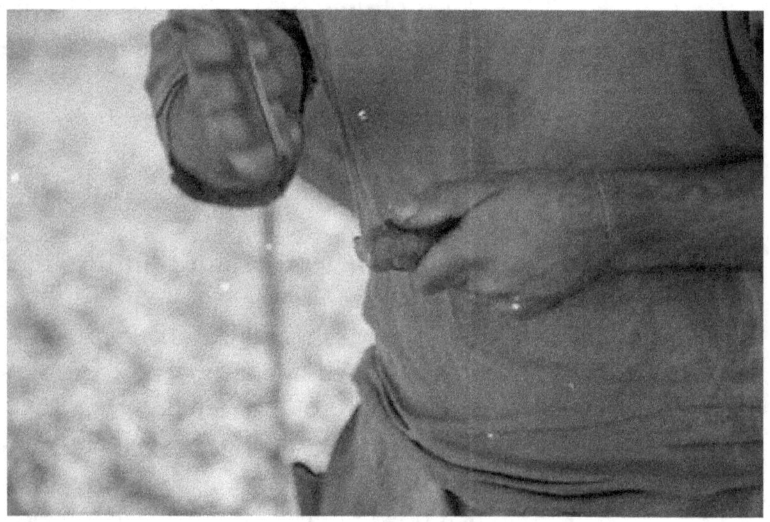

> **Flint & Hardened Steel -** is a method for making fire that is almost as old as man himself. This is a

difficult method of making fire that requires plenty of practice before it can be useful in a survival situation. A steel bladed knife is something everyone should carry with them when entering the wilderness. If flint can be found, the two devices can be sued together to create a shower of sparks; with any luck a spark will catch the ball of tinder and begin the fire making process. You must aim the sparks at the tinder for this method to work.

Friction Based

The methods featured in this category are designed to generate heat through the process of creating friction between two separate objects. Most of these methods feature a fire drill device. Several entries in this category feature assisted means of using a fire drill that the reader may not have thought of before.

> **Hand Drill -** believe it or not, you can create a coal by "rubbing two sticks together." The coal can then be transferred to the tinder ball and coaxed into making a fire. This device consists of a straight stick used as a spindle and a hearthboard. The straight spindle stick is placed in a shallow groove on the hearthboard and spun back and forth between the palms of the hands until such a time as a coal is produced. It must then be transferred safely to the tinder and fanned into a flame.

> **Team Hand Drill -** this is basically the same as the hand drill mentioned above. The difference between the two methods is that two people take turns spinning the spindle on the hearthboard to create the coal. This allows team members to rest between turns while continuing to try and make fire. It can

also consist of one team member placing weight on the top of the spindle stick while the other team member spins it back and forth; the additional pressure should create more friction if done properly.

➢ **Thong Hand Drill -** this device is a hand drill with cordage tied to the top of the spindle stick. This cordage has two holes on opposite sides of the stick that are to be used by the thumbs to hold downward pressure on the spindle as it is rotated to make fire.

➢ **Shoe Hand Drill -** this is the traditional hand drill operated between the soles of shoes. Shoes are removed from the feet and held in each hand with the soles facing the spindle. The shoes are then pressed to the spindle and used to conduct the rotating action; this will save wear and tear on the palms of your hands and should make the process easier to achieve.

➢ **Collapsible Hand Drill -** is a traditional hand drill that has been separated into two pieces for ease of transport. The two pieces are joined by a sleeve made of bamboo, rubber tubing, or anything that will join the members without allowing them to separate while in use.

➢ **Miniature Hand Drill -** it is often easier to find small straight sticks than it is to find longer sticks to use as spindles. Miniature hand drills are easier to fabricate out of natural materials, but they may be somewhat more difficult to use.

➢ **Thong Fire Drill -** this device is similar to the hand drill; it requires a straight spindle stick, a hearthboard, a length of cordage, and a pivot block. The spindle is placed in the shallow hole of the hearthboard and held in place on top by the pivot block. Cordage is then wrapped around the midsection of the spindle and used to conduct the rotating process by pulling the cordage back and forth in opposite directions.

> **Fire Bow Drill** - this is the item featured in the image that accompanies this section. It is very similar to the Thong Fire Drill mentioned directly above, the biggest difference is that each end of the cordage is tied to a third stick, creating a bow which is then used to rotate the spindle stick until a coal is created.

> **Fire Bow Drill (Two Stick Hearthboard)** - is the same as the method mentioned above only using a hearthboard created by joining two similar sized sticks together, in parallel fashion so the gap between the two can be used as the shallow groove for the spindle to be rotated in. Be careful is using this method as there is a chance the coal could fall through the gap and ignite any combustible material that might be underneath the hearthboard.

> **Fire Bow Drill (Natural Hearthboard)** - this is the same as the two mentioned directly above. The hearthboard in this case is a natural piece of wood with a crack, crevice, or groove already present. If you can find a hearthboard of this nature you won't have to carve the groove in it yourself before using.

> **Friction Fire Drill (Fungus Hearthboard)** - friction fire drill refers to any of the fire drills mentioned above. The fungus hearthboard is the biggest difference. Tinder Fungus is a woody plant that often grows on trees, and Artist's Conk which also grows on trees, are two types of fungus that can

be dried out and used as a hearthboard for any of the fire drills featured in this section.

➤ **Friction Fire Drill (Stone Hearthboard) -** this is another method of using the drills featured in this section. Finding a stone with a shallow hole/groove the size of your spindle may be difficult at best, but it is a method for making fire if one can be found.

➤ **Fire Bow Drill (Bamboo) -** this is the traditional fire drill fabricated out of dried bamboo, which makes for a great friction material. Hand drills, bows and hearthboards can all be made from dried bamboo if available.

➤ **Fire Bow Drill (Collapsible) -** this device is the same as the traditional fire bow drill, it's just made from several parts that must be held together with a tight sleeve when placed into use. Collapsible models are easier to transport but may be more difficult to use effectively for making a fire.

➤ **Fire Bow Drill (Miniature) -** the same as the traditional fire bow drill but on a miniature scale. This device is much easier to stow away and transport, but it can be somewhat difficult to use. A small fire bow drill set may not cause the operator to tire as easily, but again, the size of the system may hinder fire making progress.

➤ **Fire Bow Drill (Team) -** this device is slightly larger than the traditional fire bow drill. The team consists of at least 3 people; one holds the spindle stick upright and steady, the other two face each other on opposite ends of the bow and pull back and forth to generate the friction required to create a coal.

➤ **Hand Drill (Mouth Assisted) -** similar to using the hand drill; the biggest difference will be holding the pivot block in the mouth to keep the spindle stick sturdy and apply downward pressure during the process.

> **Fire Bow Drill (Mouth Assisted)** - uses the traditional fire bow drill and the method mentioned directly above; the pivot block is held in place with the mouth of the operator to hold the spindle straight and sturdy while applying downward pressure.

> **Pump Fire Drill** - is a device fabricated with a crossbar featuring a central hole where the spindle will rest; the hole needs to be large enough to allow the spindle to pass through it with relative ease. Cordage is then tied to the top of the spindle stick and attached to opposite ends of the crossbar. The device is operated by placing the spindle stick into a hearthboard, after which the crossbar is pumped up and down, causing the spindle to rotate rapidly and create the friction necessary to produce a coal for starting fire.

> **Additional Drill Methods** - if you have a battery operated screw gun/drill, it can be used as the rotating force for the spindle stick; you simply whittle one end of the spindle stick down so that it can be placed within the chuck of the tool and tightened in place.

> **Bamboo Fire Saw** - fire saws can be made out of several natural materials, but dried bamboo does work quite well. This device calls for cutting a bamboo stalk in half, then notching a small slot in the backside of one half. The tinder is placed in the half with the notched slot and then that half is run up and down the other half of the bamboo stalk

creating friction, which will funnel through the notch and hopefully ignite the tinder ball.

> **Fire Plow -** is another device for making a fire that is quite difficult to use. It consists of a hearthboard and a friction stick. The friction stick is plowed back and forth on the hearthboard to create a groove where friction can manufacture a coal that can be transported to a tinder ball and used to build a fire.

Firearm Based

Although this category was featured under the Conventional Fire Making methods, there were a few ancient methods for making fire with firearms that fell well within the realm of the unconventional category, primarily because these firearms are old relics that most of us will never see in our lifetimes; however, for the select few that do have them, here are the methods for making fire.

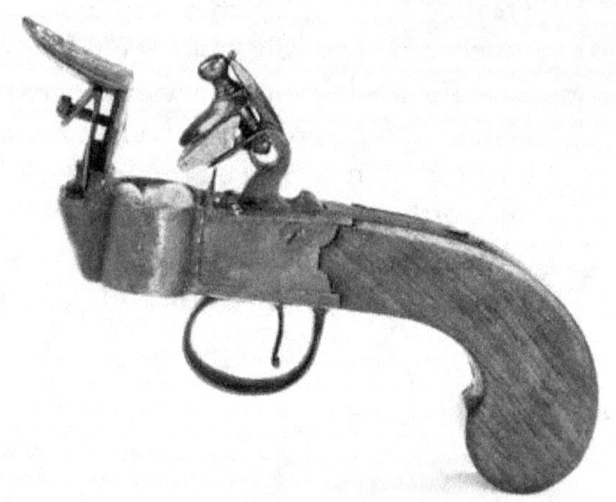

➢ **Flintlocks -** pistols or rifles can be used to get a fire going. Make sure the gun is unloaded, place a small wad of tinder in the flash pan/cup and add black powder. When you pull the trigger, the black powder should ignite and catch the wad of tinder on fire; this will need to be transferred to a large bundle of tinder and used to get kindling for the fire started.

➢ **Tinder Pistols -** like the one depicted in the image above, were designed for the specific purpose of starting a fire. They had all the mechanisms of a flintlock pistol except for the barrel. The process for using it is the same as described for flintlocks.

Fire as a Survival Skill

Making fire in a survival situation is seldom an easy task to achieve, especially if you have limited resources at your immediate disposal. Being able to build a fire is an important skill set that could literally be the difference between life and death.

When putting together GO bags and Emergency Preparedness Kits, it is recommended that you have no less than three methods for making fire included at all times. The easiest methods for making fire should always be used first and foremost until such a time as they are no longer useful, such as a disposable lighter.

Several of the unconventional methods for making fire that are mentioned in this book are extremely exhausting; they consume an enormous amount of energy, so if you cannot readily replace that lost energy, you could be in trouble. You should strive to expend less energy than you are able to replace in every aspect of survival.

In a survival situation, fire provides us with the ability

to accomplish many of the other tasks we will also need in order to make it out alive. If you really want to get a firsthand look at how important this skill is, spend an hour outside in the backyard during the middle of the night, after the sun goes down and temperatures begin to drop, with nothing more than the clothes on your back. It will not be an easy task to accomplish and you may not even last the entire hour before seeking shelter and the warmth inside.

The methods mentioned in this book are just that; they are ways that man has made fire throughout the centuries and continues to make fire to this day. These entries do not provide an in depth explanation as to how each method works, or what the success rates are. These entries are to give you ideas on how fire can be created using a variety of tools and materials.

Readers should strive to have conventional fire making methods available to them at all times, even in their EDC kits. They should also practice making fire using unconventional tools and methods as these are the ways that our early ancestors had to get by in order to survive, and they may be the very means by which we have to survive should we find ourselves stranded in the wilderness without conventional means.

Unconventional fire making methods should be practiced repeatedly and continuously as they are perishable skills that you may forget over time. Continued practice keeps the method fresh and helps build muscle memory for future excursions.

ALL RIGHTS RESERVED. No part of this publication may be reproduced or transmitted in any form whatsoever, electronic, or mechanical, including photocopying, recording, or by any informational storage or retrieval system without express written, dated and signed permission from the author.

DISCLAIMER AND/OR LEGAL NOTICES: Every effort has been made to accurately represent this book and it's potential. Results vary with every individual, and your results may or may not be different from those depicted. No promises, guarantees or warranties, whether stated or implied, have been made that you will produce any specific result from this book. Your efforts are individual and unique, and may vary from those shown. Your success depends on your efforts, background and motivation. The material in this publication is provided for educational and informational purposes only. Use of the programs, advice, and information contained in this book is at the sole discretion and risk of the reader

www.ingramcontent.com/pod-product-compliance
Lightning Source LLC
Chambersburg PA
CBHW070050260726
48658CB00002B/824